The Cat in the Hat's Learning Library

The editors would like to thank
BARBARA KIEFER, PhD,
Charlotte S. Huck Professor of Children's Literature,
The Ohio State University, and
THEODORE CHAO, PhD,
Department of Teaching and Learning,
The Ohio State University,
for their assistance in the preparation of this book.

Visit us on the Web!
Seussville.com
rhcbooks.com

Educators and librarians, for a variety of teaching tools, visit us at RHTeachersLibrarians.com

*Library of Congress Cataloging-in-Publication Data*
Names: Worth, Bonnie, author. | Ruiz, Aristides, illustrator. | Mathieu, Joe, illustrator.
Title: Happy pi day to you! / by Bonnie Worth ; illustrated by Aristides Ruiz and Joe Mathieu. |
Cat in the Hat's learning library.
Description: First edition. | New York : Random House Children's Books, [2020] |
Series: The Cat in the Hat's Learning library | Audience: Ages 5–8.
Identifiers: LCCN 2018046800 | ISBN 978-0-525-57993-9 (trade) | ISBN 978-0-525-57994-6 (lib. bdg.)
Subjects: LCSH: Pi—Juvenile literature. | Circle-squaring—Juvenile literature. |
Mathematics—Juvenile literature. | Cat in the Hat (Fictitious character)—Juvenile literature.
Classification: LCC QA484 .W67 2020 | DDC 513.2—dc23

Printed in China

10 9 8 7 6 5 4 3

First Edition

# Happy Pi Day to You!

by Bonnie Worth

illustrated by Aristides Ruiz and Joe Mathieu

The Cat in the Hat's Learning Library®

Random House 🏠 New York

Hurray for Pi Day!
Would you like to find out
just what this day means?
What Pi Day is about?

It is all about circles
and measuring fun.
So put on your Pi Hats!
Let's start, everyone!

We begin with a circle,
the shape of a pie.
Look around you and name
all the circles you spy.

Yes, circles surround us
wherever we are—
from pennies to pizzas
to wheels on a car.

Some circles we see
look pretty flat . . .

PIZZA

PIZZA

9

. . . but other ones look
a bit different than that.

You'll find circles in cylinders,
like this tube that is blue.
And spheres—like this ball—
have a circle shape, too.

cylinder
(SIH-lin-der)

sphere
(SFEER)

To draw a flat circle
(one of my best tricks),
all you need is some string
and a couple of sticks.

string

sticks

Tie the string to two sticks.
Now, plant one in the ground.
Use the other to poke
lots of dots all around.

A circle's a shape
made of dot after dot,
equal distance away
from one middle spot.

Link the dots and you'll get
a word of great size.
Say cir-cum-fer-ence
(ser-KUM-frents).
(It may take a few tries!)

circumference

Cut the circle in half
with a single straight line.
That line is called diameter
(dy-AM-uh-ter).
Can you draw one like mine?

The length of the string
there beneath Sally's hand
measures half the diameter—
do you understand?

We call this length radius
(RAY-dee-us).

Mark it with an **r**.

Are you getting all this?

Are you with me so far?

r
(radius)

diameter

Now, take the circumference—
oh, let's call it **C**—
and divide by diameter,
which we will call **d**.

How do we divide?
You're a smart one to ask!
I have a new trick that
will help with the task.

d
(diameter)

C
(circumference)

Take a tube made of cardboard
just like this one, and then
a wide piece of ribbon
and your marking pen.

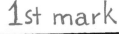

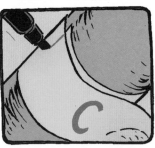

Wrap the ribbon 'round the tube
and mark the length with a **C**.
Then lay it across the top
and mark that length with a **d**.

2nd mark

Measure out three **d**-lengths
and then you will see,
three folds of **d**-lengths—
*plus a bit more*—equals **C**.

1st fold

2nd fold

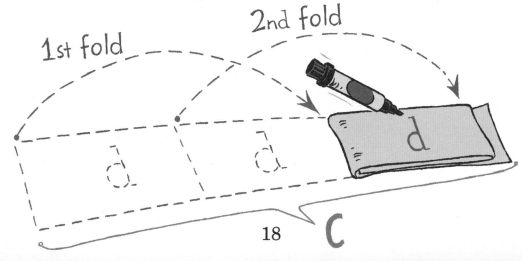

No matter what size
your tube is, I'll bet
three lengths *plus a bit more*
is the answer you'll get.

d = diameter

d

d

d

d

C =
circumference

C

**C** divided by **d**
equals three whole times—plus.
That's division for you—
you can take it from us!

d d d d

This number that is
"a bit more" than three
is looooooong, so we give it
a short name, you see.

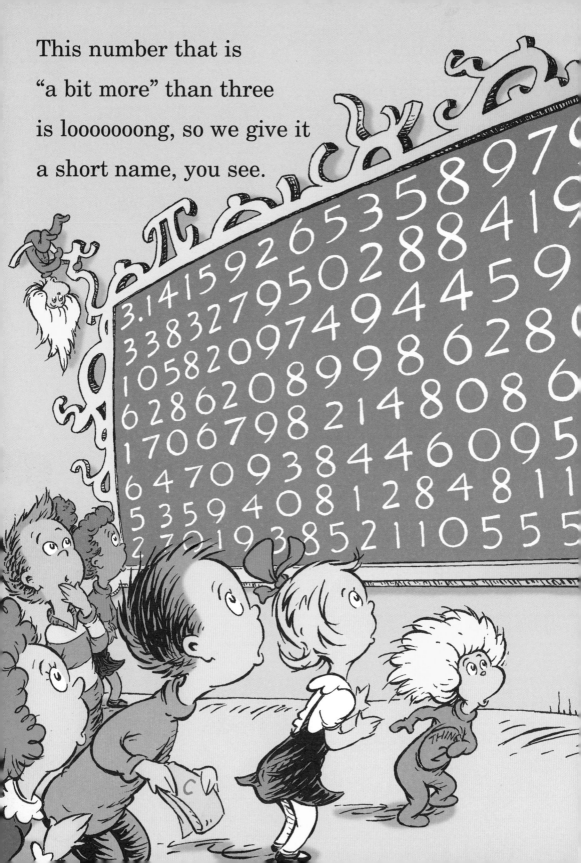

π

3.14159265358979
33832795028841
10582097494459
62862089986280
17067982148086
64709384460095
35940812848111
27019385211055

3238462642338462643841640
7169399375
30781640
348253421
1328230 6
058223172
745028410
96446229...

We call it pi—
a name short and sweet.
Because writing it out
is a difficult feat!

The number goes on
and on, as you see.
In fact, it goes on until . . .

. . . infinity!

Another name that folks
have used to call pi
is irrational, or crazy.
And now you know why.

We can spell the word *pi*
with a *p* and an *i*,
or else use a mark.
Let's give it a try.

The mark looks like this: π
It's from long, long ago.
It's the Greek letter pi—
a good symbol to know.

THE PI-TOSS GAME ⟶

1. DRAW **4** LINES **2** TOOTHPICK LENGTHS APART.
2. RANDOMLY SCATTER TOOTHPICKS.
3. SEPARATE AND COUNT ALL TOOTHPICKS TOUCHING A LINE.
4. DIVIDE THE TOTAL NUMBER OF TOOTHPICKS BY THE NUMBER OF TOOTHPICKS TOUCHING A LINE. THE RESULT CLOSEST TO PI (3.14...) WINS!!

C divided by **d**

is a theorem (THEE-uh-rum), we say.

What's that, you ask?

I'll explain, if I may.

*Theorem*'s a word
that smart people like you
can use to describe
an idea that is true.

**C** divided by **d**
equals pi, as you see.
Forever and always—
this always will be!

On Pi Day, it is
a good bit of fun
to honor pi pioneers
and all they have done.

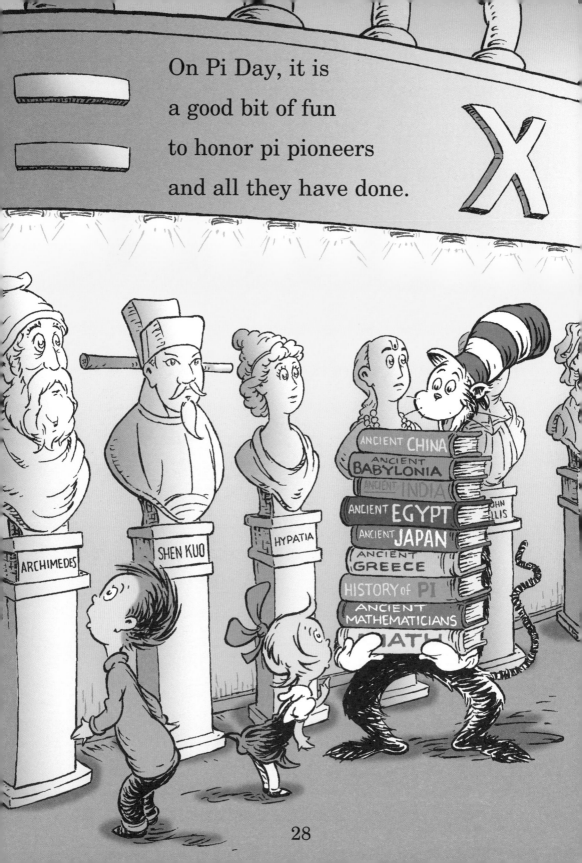

Did cave people measure?
They took a wild guess.
I do that myself
sometimes, I'll confess.

When people began
to build and to trade,
universal measurements
had to be made.

Egyptians measured with cubits—
a unit that goes
from middle finger tips
to the crease of elbows.

But since arm lengths differed,
they learned the neat trick
of making a universal
measuring stick.

Using pi to measure,
they built pyramids for tombs
with secret passageways
and underground rooms.

cubit

cubit stick

In 250 BC,
a Greek good at math
put on his pi hat
and went down the pi path.

Ancient Greeks loved their circles.
Using pi they built lots
of arches and arenas
in big public spots.

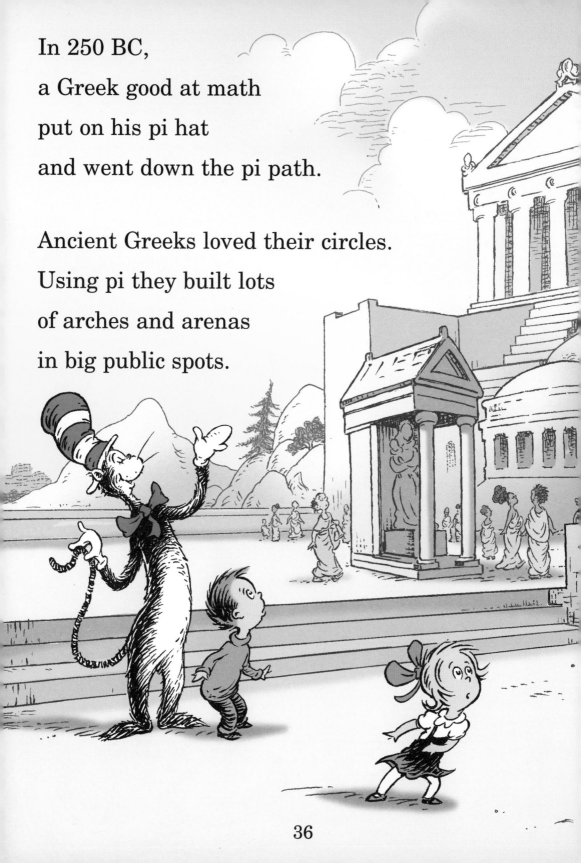

ARCHIMEDES

It's people like these who gave pi its start. They've helped us to be so much smarter than smart.

We're feeling so smart and so happy, I'll say to one and to all—

# HAVE A HAPPY PI DAY!

# GLOSSARY

**Circumference:** The measurement around a circle.

**Confess:** To admit something with some reluctance.

**Cylinder:** A solid figure with parallel sides and a circular top.

**Diameter:** A straight line that passes through the center of a circle, going from one side to the other.

**Divide:** To separate into smaller, equal parts.

**Infinity:** Something that never ends.

**Irrational number:** A number that goes on forever without repeating a pattern.

**Measure:** To figure out the size, amount, or degree of something by using an instrument with marked units, such as a ruler or a thermometer.

**Method:** An orderly way of doing something, such as solving a math problem, performing an experiment, or even cleaning your room.

**Parallel:** Side-by-side lines that have the same distance between them and never touch, even if extended infinitely.

**Radius:** A straight line that runs from the center of a circle to its circumference, or edge.

**Sphere:** A round figure shaped like a ball.

**Universal:** A thing that is understood around the world or by all people in a given group.

# PI DAY RESOURCES

Here are some suggested resources to create your own Pi Day celebration in your home, school, or community:

## Pi Day Origins

The holiday started in San Francisco in 1988 when Larry Shaw, also known as the Prince of Pi, late physicist and technical curator of the San Francisco Exploratorium museum, founded Pi Day. Today, it is celebrated live and online around the world. The official date is March 14, and for good reason. When you write out the date in numerals, like this—3.14—you get the number pi! The next best thing to going to the Exploratorium and participating in the hands-on exhibits is to visit the website exploratorium.edu/pi and enjoy a piece of the pi. Search for "Pi Toss" and you'll find directions for playing the same fun game—using chips or toothpicks—as the kids on page 25.

## Pi Day Challenge

This clever site, refreshed every year for Pi Day, provides puzzles to solve so that you, too, can be a Pi Day Genius. But beware! Not all of these puzzles are as easy as pie. Some are real stumpers. Do you dare take on the challenge? pidaychallenge.com

## Pi Day for Teachers

Visit this site to discover an entire menu of activities, puzzles, jokes, and games submitted by teachers, students, and "everyday people." From making paper chains representing each digit of pi to having a Pi Day scavenger hunt, you can have lots of "fun that is funny" (to quote the Cat in the Hat). piday.org/2008/2008-pi-day-activities-for-teachers

## Number Lovers

This site offers over 50 crafts, recipes, games, songs, and art projects to help kids understand all about pi. So that kids will get the connection between pi and pie, there are activities centered around pies, measuring a pie's diameter and circumference, and dividing that pie into equal slices . . . to eat—all the better to celebrate Pi Day. teachpi.org/activities

# INDEX

The Cat in the Hat's Learning Library

The Cat in the Hat's Learning Library

The Cat in the Hat's Learning Library

The Cat in the Hat's Learning Library

The Cat in the Hat's Learning Library

The Cat in the Hat's Learning Library

The Cat in the Hat's Learning Library

The Cat in the Hat's Learning Library

The Cat in the Hat's Learning Library

The Cat in the Hat's Learning Library

The Cat in the Hat's Learning Library

The Cat in the Hat's Learning Library

The Cat in the Hat's Learning Library

The Cat in the Hat's Learning Library

The Cat in the Hat's Learning Library

The Cat in the Hat's Learning Library

The Cat in the Hat's Learning Library